The
Aztec

by William Caper

TABLE OF CONTENTS

INTRODUCTION

Imagine taking a trip to Mexico City, the **capital** of Mexico. You will see **ruins**, or remains, of buildings from long ago. A people called the Aztec made these buildings. Before Christopher Columbus sailed to America, the Aztec ruled a powerful **empire** in Mexico. Their capital was a large city that stood where Mexico City is today.

▲ Mexico City today

The Aztec Empire came to a sudden end in the 1500s, when it was **conquered**, or taken over, by the Spanish.

How did the Aztec Empire grow to be so strong? What was life like there? Why did the Spanish conquer the Aztec? Look for the answers to those questions as you read.

▲ Aztec ruins in Mexico City

THE RISE OF THE AZTEC EMPIRE 1200–1399

The name *Aztec* is used for the people who built the city of Tenochtitlán (tay-nahch-teet-LAHN) in the Valley of Mexico. There is a **legend**, or story mixed with fact and fiction, about how the Aztec came to be.

The legend says that **ancestors** of the Aztec came from a place north of the Valley of Mexico. Those ancestors moved from place to place for many years. Finally, they settled in the Valley of Mexico.

The Aztec came to the Valley of Mexico in the 1200s. At that time, they were very poor. They had no home and they had no land. The other people living in the valley did not like them. The Aztec tried to live near those people, but they were driven away.

The Aztec built a city they ▶ called Tenochtitlán in the Valley of Mexico. The arrow shows where the Aztec came into the valley from the north.

Tenochtitlán

Bay of Campeche

North America

South America

Pacific Ocean

SCALE OF MILES
0   50   100

Finally, in 1325, the Aztec found a marshy island in the middle of a lake. They made this wet, grassy island their home. They began to build a city they called Tenochtitlán.

▲ According to Aztec legend, their war god told them to search for a special place to build a city. He told them to look for an eagle standing on a cactus and eating a snake. When the people arrived on the island in the lake, that's exactly what they saw. They built Tenochtitlán on this island.

At first, life was very hard in Tenochtitlán. The swampy land was hard to build on. There was not a lot of clean water to drink. And the Aztec always had to be watchful. The other people in the valley still did not like them.

But the Aztec worked hard. They built huts made of straw and mud. They built small temples. They found ways to bring clean drinking water to their island city.

The Aztec built special plots of land to farm on. The plots of land were islands of soil that seemed to float on the lake. The Aztec were able to grow more food than they needed. They used the extra food to trade with other people.

▲ This is a 16th-century map of Tenochtitlán.

▲ The Aztec farmed on islands of soil called chinampas (chih-NAHM-puz). They can still be seen today in some parts of Mexico.

Tenochtitlán got bigger and bigger. The Aztec were still having problems with their neighbors. The Aztec realized they needed a leader that other people in the valley would respect.

In 1376, the Aztec chose a new king, named Acamapichtli (ah-kah-mah-PECH-tlee). His ancestors were very important people. When he became the Aztec king, the other people in the valley began to have more respect for the Aztec.

Tenochtitlán continued to grow. The Aztec brought skilled people from other places to make the city bigger.

The Aztec became better soldiers. They helped other groups in war. People in the valley respected them more. The Aztec grew in power.

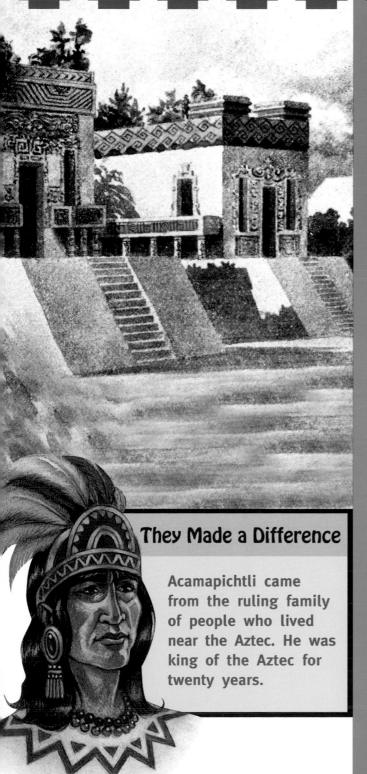

It's a Fact

Archaeologists (ar-kee-AH-luh-jists) dig up and study the remains of people and objects from long ago. In Mexico City, archaeologists have dug up the ruins of the Aztec's Great Temple. They found about 6,000 different objects. The objects include pottery, jewelry, statues, and the bones of animals and people.

They Made a Difference

Acamapichtli came from the ruling family of people who lived near the Aztec. He was king of the Aztec for twenty years.

THE GREAT AZTEC CIVILIZATION 1400–1519

By the early 1400s, Tenochtitlán had grown into a strong **city-state**. A city-state is a city that is like its own country. It rules the land around it.

There were other city-states in the Valley of Mexico. Tenochtitlán joined two other city-states. Together, the three city-states fought against and conquered other people in the valley.

In 1440, Montezuma (mahn-teh-ZOO-muh) I became the Aztec king. He was a strong leader and a powerful warrior. He ruled from 1440 to 1469.

Montezuma I helped the Aztec conquer people beyond the Valley of Mexico. The Aztec kings after Montezuma I won even more land for the Aztec.

They Made a Difference

Montezuma I was also known as "Montezuma the Great." He helped the Aztec Empire get much larger. He helped build special waterways to bring fresh water to Tenochtitlán.

◄ By the early 1500s, there were as many as 300,000 people living in or near Tenochtitlán.

Raised roads made of soil went from Tenochtitlán to the land around it. There were streets and canals in the city. People could travel by land or by water. The city was filled with houses, palaces, temples, and **pyramids**. The Aztec had ball courts and even a zoo. There was a huge market visited by people from all over the Aztec Empire.

The Aztec conquered more and more land. Finally, their empire extended from the Gulf of Mexico to the Pacific Ocean.

THE AZTEC EMPIRE

Aztec soldiers made sure conquered people did not revolt, or go against the Aztec. Conquered people were allowed to keep their own religion and way of life. But conquered towns had to pay taxes to the Aztec. Money was not used in the Aztec Empire. Instead, people paid taxes with goods and services.

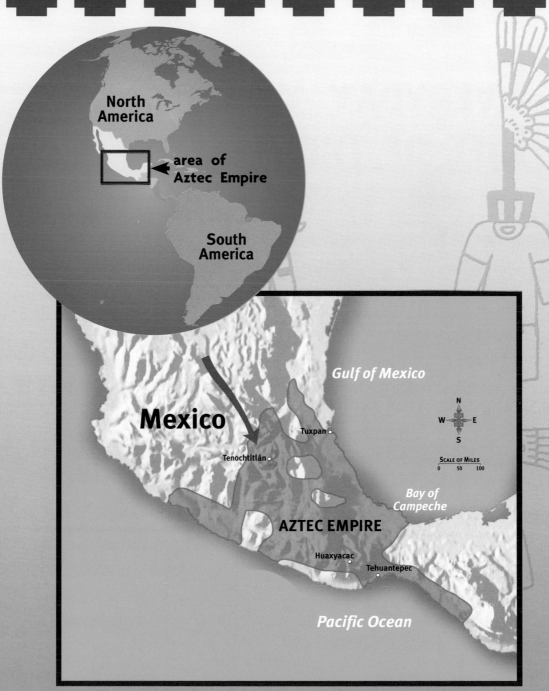

North
America

← area of
Aztec Empire

South
America

Gulf of Mexico

Mexico

Tuxpan

Tenochtitlán

N
W E
S

SCALE OF MILES
0   50   100

Bay of
Campeche

AZTEC EMPIRE

Huaxyacac

Tehuantepec

Pacific Ocean

▲ The Aztec Empire spread over 80,000 square
miles (207,200 square kilometers).

EVERYDAY LIFE OF THE AZTEC

Aztec people were separated into classes, or types. The highest class was **nobles**. They had high social rank, or position. The second highest class was commoners. Commoners were ordinary people. Most of the people were commoners.

The third class was made up of serfs. Serfs worked on land held by nobles. The lowest class was slaves. They were thought of as property. Slaves were people who had been captured in war, or had committed a crime. Some had not paid a debt they owed.

EDUCATION

Education was very important to the Aztec. There were two kinds of schools. In one kind of school, children studied history and religion. Boys learned how to farm and become soldiers. Girls were taught how to raise a family and make a good home.

The other kind of school was a school run by a temple. Temple schools taught boys to be priests or other types of leaders. Nobles often went to temple schools.

▲ daily life in Tenochtitlán

RELIGION

The Aztec believed that the gods and goddesses ruled **agriculture**, or farming. The Aztec thought it was important to please the gods in order to grow good crops.

The Aztec also believed that human hearts and blood kept their gods strong. So they made human **sacrifices**. Most of the people sacrificed were slaves or prisoners taken in war. The Aztec believed the souls of the people sacrificed would go to a special place for warriors.

HISTORICAL PERSPECTIVE

Many early people believed in human sacrifice. Today, people do not have this as part of their religion. Human sacrifice is thought of as too cruel.

◄ This picture shows an Aztec sacrifice.

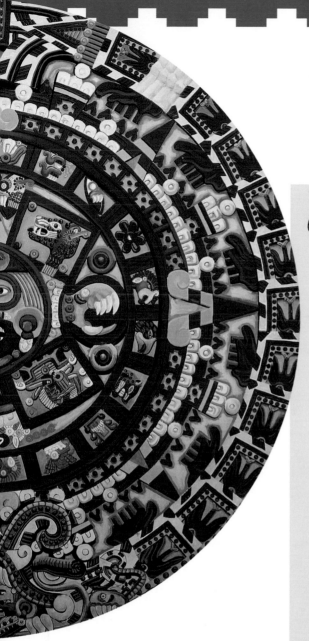

THE GOD QUETZALCOATL

Quetzalcoatl (ket-sul-kuh-WAH-tul) was a very important god of the Aztec. He was the special god of priests. The Aztec thought he invented their calendar and books. There are several **myths**, or stories, about Quetzalcoatl. One myth says that he gathered the bones of the dead. He used the bones to create the Aztec people. Quetzalcoatl was sometimes shown as a snake, and sometimes as a man with a beard.

▲ The Aztec had a 260-day religious calendar. Priests used it to decide when to plant crops or go to war.

FARMING

Most of the Aztec were farmers. Corn was the most important crop. They also grew beans, sweet potatoes, tomatoes, and squash.

Tenochtitlán had the largest market in the Americas. People went there to trade crops and other things. More than 60,000 people went to this market every day.

The Aztec did not use money. They traded things with one another. They traded feathers, animal skins, beans, rubber, and **obsidian** (ub-SIH-dee-un). Obsidian is a glass-like stone from volcanoes that the Aztec used to make weapons.

The Aztecs were the first people to make chocolate. Here an Aztec priest offers Montezuma I a chocolate drink.

WAR

The Aztec fought wars to get more land. They also fought to capture prisoners to sacrifice to their gods. Warriors who took many prisoners in battle were rewarded. They received land and jobs.

Aztec warriors carried shields made of reeds, or grasses. The shields were then covered with feathers. The warriors wore armor made of thick cotton. Their main weapon was a wooden club. The club had sharp pieces of obsidian in it. The Aztec liked the weapon because they could use it to defeat an enemy without killing him. The Aztec also used spears, and bows and arrows.

✔ POINT

Think About It

How was the world of the Aztec like our world today? How was it different?

Aztec Achievements

▲ This is a model of part of the Great Temple area.

T he Aztec did many things. They found ways to farm on islands of soil in the water. They built **terraces**, or wide steps covered with soil, on mountainsides. They farmed on the terraces. The Aztec found a way to bring water to crops where there was little or no water before. They built beautiful temples and other buildings.

The Aztec wrote poetry and stories. They also wrote about their battles and other things that happened to them.

THE GREAT TEMPLE

The Aztec built walled areas for their religious ceremonies. The most important area was the Great Temple area in Tenochtitlán.

The Great Temple area was as long as four football fields. It had three large pyramids and six small pyramids. Many priests lived there.

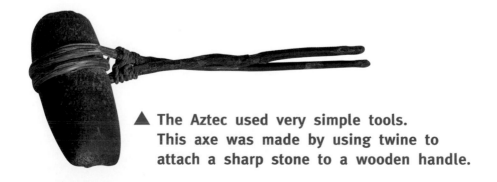

▲ The Aztec used very simple tools. This axe was made by using twine to attach a sharp stone to a wooden handle.

WRITING

Not all people living at the time of the Aztec had a form of writing. The Aztec did. They used a kind of writing that had been around for a thousand years. It is called pictographic (pik-tuh-GRA-fik) writing. Pictographic writing uses pictures instead of letters and words. Some pictures show ideas. Other pictures stand for sounds.

The Aztec used their writing to tell about their history. They also wrote about their gods and goddesses.

MATH

The Aztec had a number system. Our number system is based on the number 10. The Aztec number system was based on the number 20.

The numbers 1 to 19 were written using dots. Glyphs (GLIFS), or pictures, were used for larger numbers based on groups of 20. For example, a flag stood for 20. A feather meant 400, or 20 groups of 20.

It's a Fact

The Aztec spoke a language that is like languages spoken today by some Native Americans.

▲ These are symbols for days on the
Aztec calendar.

THE SPANISH CONQUEST 1519–1521

Hernando Cortés (air-NAHN-doh kor-TEZ) was a Spanish soldier and explorer. In 1519, he sailed for Mexico with eleven ships and 650 soldiers. Cortés and his men reached the east coast of Mexico. They fought and defeated Native American armies there.

The Native Americans had many more soldiers than Cortés did. Even so, Cortés and his men beat the Native Americans in battle. The Spanish had cannons. They also had horses. The Spanish soldiers wore metal armor. The Native Americans had never seen those things.

The Aztec king Montezuma II heard about the Spanish soldiers. He heard about their cannons and odd clothing. He thought the Spanish soldiers might be gods.

Montezuma II sent gold and other gifts to the Spanish. He hoped the gifts would please them and they would go away. Instead, the gifts made Cortés think that the Aztec had more treasure. In August 1519, Cortés and his soldiers started to march toward Tenochtitlán.

Hernando Cortés

▲ Hernando Cortés and Tlaxcaltecs soldiers marched to Tenochtitlán.

On the march, Cortés met Native Americans who had been conquered by the Aztec. Those Native Americans hated the Aztec. The Aztec had been very cruel to them. So the Native Americans joined Cortés's army. The Spanish army grew bigger and bigger as it marched toward Tenochtitlán. In November, Cortés and his men went into the city.

▲ This is a 17th-century painting of Cortés meeting Aztec soldiers.

Cortés saw at once that the Aztec had more soldiers. He knew he would not be able to win if the Aztec decided to fight. So he took Montezuma II prisoner. He said that the king would stay safe if the Aztec did not fight. At first, Cortés's plan worked. But it didn't work for very long.

Primary Source

Cortés wrote about being in Tenochtitlán. He knew the city was on an island. He was afraid that he and his men might be trapped on the island.

"...as soon as I had entered... I made great haste to build four brigantines (boats), which were soon finished, and were large enough to take ashore three hundred men and the horses, whenever it should become necessary."

27

About six months later, the Aztec started to fight the Spanish. The Aztec and the Spanish fought for about six weeks. Then, the Spanish tried to sneak out of Tenochtitlán at night. The Aztec caught them. Hundreds of Spanish soldiers were killed. The Spanish called it "la noche triste" (LAH NOH-chay TREE-stay). This means "the sad night."

The Aztec might have killed all the Spanish in this battle. But the Native Americans who had been helping the Spanish stopped the Aztec. They saved the lives of many Spanish soldiers. Cortés lived and escaped from Tenochtitlán.

Montezuma II, the Aztec king, died a few days after the battle.

In December 1520, Cortés came back to Tenochtitlán. He brought Spanish soldiers and a large army of Native Americans.

Cortés's army camped around the city. The Aztec inside could not get food and water. They grew weak from hunger, thirst, and sickness. Finally, on August 13, 1521, Tenochtitlán gave up. The Aztec Empire had come to an end.

The Spanish destroyed Tenochtitlán. They began to build a new city in its place. This city would become Mexico City. The Spanish also built cities in other parts of Mexico.

Mexico was renamed New Spain. Cortés ruled New Spain for a short time. He started new cities and continued to explore New Spain.

This picture of "the sad night" is
from a book written in the 1500s. ▼

▽ POINT

Talk About It

What impressed you the most about the Aztec?
Share your thoughts with others who have read the book.

CONCLUSION

The Aztec built and ruled a great empire in what became the country of Mexico. Their capital was a large city that stood where Mexico City is today.

Use the time line to tell the story of the Aztec.

TIME LINE OF THE AZTEC EMPIRE

1200s — The Aztec arrive in the Valley of Mexico.

1325 — Tenochtitlán is founded.

1440 — Montezuma I becomes king of the Aztec.

1469 — Montezuma I dies.

1502 — Montezuma II becomes king of the Aztec.

1519 — Hernando Cortés arrives in Mexico.

1520 — Montezuma II dies.

1521 — The Spanish conquer Tenochtitlán.

GLOSSARY

agriculture   (A-grih-kul-cher) farming and raising animals (page 16)

ancestor   (AN-ses-ter) a person in a family who lived a very long time ago (page 4)

archaeologist   (ar-kee-AH-luh-jist) a person who studies the remains of things and people from long ago (page 9)

capital   (KA-pih-tul) the city where a country's government is located (page 2)

city-state   (SIH-tee-state) a city that has its own government and controls the territory around it (page 10)

conquered   (KAHN-kerd) taken over by force (page 3)

empire   (EM-pire) a large land that is ruled by one nation (page 2)

legend   (LEH-jend) a story that is told over and over, which may be partly true (page 4)

myth   (MITH) a story that tells about ancient history, gods, ancestors, or heroes (page 17)

noble   (NOH-bul) a person of high birth or rank (page 14)

obsidian   (ub-SIH-dee-un) hard, black, glass-like stone that comes from volcanoes (page 18)

pyramid   (PEER-uh-mid) a building that has a square base and four triangular sides that meet at a point on top (page 12)

ruin   (ROO-in) what's left after something has been destroyed (page 2)

sacrifice   (SA-krih-fise) the act of killing a human or animal and offering it to a god (page 16)

terrace   (TAIR-us) a flat step or area built on the side of a hill, and filled with soil (page 21)

INDEX